19 Budget Hacks for College Students:

How to Live on $15 a Day Without Dying

By Richard Glen

Published by LearnU.org © 2015

Introduction

I spent many years as a college student, as you may already know from my last book, *19 High-Impact Study Hacks: Learn the Techniques Top Students Use to Get Amazing Grades and Cut Study Time in Half.*

Much of my time in school was spent on a budget that hardly afforded me two nickels to rub together after I bought food and paid my bills. There were more times than I can count when the money to pay for my meals came from my couch cushions, under my car seats or from trading in video games. I did what I had to in order to get by, but I wish I'd had more money-savvy tools in my toolbox during those days.

Since the days of skipping meals and wearing holey clothes in a cold, sparsely furnished apartment are behind me, I figured I would share some of the hacks I used to stay within my budget and some of the things I wish I would have known about.

The hacks that I've whipped up for you will help you live your life on a budget—with an emphasis on the word "live." When implementing some of the tips and tricks in the chapters of this book, you'll really be able focus on your studies and enjoy your time in college rather than have your focus shifted to how much or little is in your bank account.

In other words, you'll be able to survive. Obviously, you're not going to be buying yachts with this budget. But you'll be comfortable.

My intent is to help you get a little breathing room, to come up with a good plan.

I hope you'll give a few of my suggestions a try and that you find them useful. They've saved me from going hungry and becoming homeless more than a time or two, that's for sure. I'd love to hear your suggestions or success stories, so feel free to send them my way via email at admin@learnu.org.

You can always stop by Learnu.org for a chat and to see what else we are working on too!

Good luck and happy budgeting!

Thanks for reading!

Richard

Table of Contents

Before we get started...

As a small token of thanks for buying this book, I'd like to offer a free bonus gift exclusive to my readers:

This action-packed PDF is called *Stress & Students* and has tons of valuable lessons for students who sometimes feel overwhelmed with school. These tips honestly helped keep me sane when I was going through grad school.

In this FREE bonus, you'll learn:
- How to stay focused
- How to keep things in perspective
- What stuff is worth stressing over
- What stuff *isn't* worth stressing over
- How to manage stress when it occurs
- And much more!

You can download the free gift here:
http://www.learnu.org/student-stress/

Chapter 1: Let's talk about what living on $15/day actually means.

How to Live on $15/Day

When I say "…live on $15 per day," I mean *everything*. Rent. Utilities. Food. Fun. Everything.

And I'm not going to beat around the bush here: it's not easy.

Living on $15/day is a pretty tight budget, and I really, really want you to remember something as you're reading this book: you're going to have to make some sacrifices.

So before we even get started with the awesome hacks in the following chapters, I thought it'd be criminal not to give you an introductory chapter on budgeting for a $15/day lifestyle.

What is a budget?

At its simplest, a budget is just a list of your expenses. It includes both your fixed expenses (stuff like rent and food) and discretionary expenses (pretty much anything you don't absolutely *need*, like going to the movies).

Ideally, your total budget should be *less* than your income. If you don't have any income, you want your budget to be at least 1/6th of your savings (or six months of living expenses), which will give you some time to figure out how to get some money coming in.

If you combine the two, a budget tracks your expenses and compares them against your income. It records money in vs. money out.

And it doesn't have to be fancy. It can be a few lines in a notebook, or you can use any number of free tools out there (I'll show you some below).

What does a $15/day budget look like?

The idea of this book is to live on $15 a day. **That translates to $450 per month.**

That includes *everything*: rent, food, utilities… everything. So, to really make this book work for you, you need to be earning at least $450 per month, or you need to have $2,700 in savings.

Of course, if you have more in savings, you'll be more comfortable. Based on a $15/day budget, here's how much money you'd need to live for different lengths of time:

- 4 months (1 semester): $1,800
- 6 months (1 semester + a break): $2,700
- 9 months (1 school year): $4,050
- 12 months (2 semesters + 2 breaks): $5,400

Assuming you make minimum wage and can stay with your parents (or someone) over a break, you should be able to save $5,400, since it would take about 18 weeks (about the length of a full summer break and a full winter break combined).

What if that's not an option for you?

First, that's totally cool. Working and saving won't be an option for everyone. For example, maybe you can't stay with your parents, or you already live on your own. In that case, you probably need to work instead of living off savings.

So here's (roughly) the number of hours you'd need to work to live on this budget with different hourly wage rates (assuming an average tax rate):

- $7.25/hr (average minimum wage in the U.S.): 22.25 hours per week
- $9.00/hr (minimum wage in California): 16.25 hours per week
- $12.00/hr (rate a decent entry-level or manual labor job): 13.5 hours per week
- $15.00/hr (rate for a great entry-level or manual labor job): 10.75 hours per week

So how do we achieve this? How do we actually live on $15 per day?

Here's a very basic budget to use as a guideline. Any of these numbers can be adjusted based on your specific situation. For example, you may find super cheap rent somewhere, so you can afford to increase your food budget. Or, perhaps, your landlord pays for your electricity, which means your utility budget could be lower, and your rent could be higher.

You get the idea.

Sample Monthly Budget

Here's a very simple breakdown of what such a budget might look like (remember, we'll be helping you hack all these things below):

- Rent: $250
- Utilities: $50
- Internet: $30
- Phone: $0
- Food: $80
- Fun: $20
- Miscellaneous: $20

Sample Weekly Budget

On a weekly basis, this is what your budget might look like. I'm leaving off the monthly payments here, since they're, well, paid monthly and not weekly. And remember this is just a sample. Things can be adjusted.

- **Food: $18.38** (includes tax; sample prices taken from Jewel Osco in Chicago in 2015):
    - 2lbs rice: $1.99
    - 5 cans black beans: $4.45
    - 2 bag frozen, chopped broccoli: $3.58
    - 2lbs chicken thighs: $3.98
    - 1 bottle teriyaki sauce: $2.09
    - 1 bag frozen stir fry vegetables: $2.29
- **Fun: $5**
    - Seeing a student-produced play at a university theater: $0
    - 3 pickup basketball games: $0

- o 1 movie night with friends (watching a documentary on YouTube; someone brings popcorn): $0
- o 1 coffee with a cute gal/guy: $5
- **Emergency plunger: $7**
  - o Beans have a lot of fiber, you know

I know that looks crazy, but hopefully it doesn't look *too* crazy. We'll cover a lot of stuff in more detail in the following chapters, but it should be clear that you can live comfortably on $15/day. At the very least, you won't die.

In fact, here's my guarantee: if you die following this budget, shoot me an email, and I'll give you your money back!

All jokes aside, I just want to take a second to reiterate this point: **to live on a budget like this, you'll have to make some sacrifices.**

In the chapters that follow, I'll do my best to give you amazing money-saving hacks, but I'll also do my best to seriously outline the sacrifices you'll have to make to save that money.

At the end of the day, though, it's very possible to live on $15 per day, especially if you're a student.

A short note on income…

This book isn't about generating income for yourself. If you're interested in that, there are plenty of other amazing books out there (not to mention a plethora of fantastic blogs).

However, I wanted to take two super quick seconds to point out that no matter what your budget is, you're going to need to either (1) have some savings or (2) have some money coming in.

I, personally, am a big fan of the side hustle: a gig you create for yourself that lets you control your own schedule. For example, you could start a blog online. Or you could do a bit of freelance writing. Or you could create a small lawn-mowing business. Or you could walk around to your local businesses and offer to wash their windows.

A side hustle can be literally anything, and it can either provide you with your whole budget or give you more breathing room.

Alternatively, to live on this budget, you really only need one small part-time job. For most people, a part-time minimum wage job will be enough to support one adult on this budget (this book assumes that you're only supporting yourself).

Whether it's a gig of your own or a part-time job, working part-time will be invaluable after you finish school and are looking for full-time employment or starting your own business. So don't be afraid to get out there and look for some money!

Enough jabber! Let's get to these hacks!

Food Hacks

Food... The struggle is real! There's no denying that food is expensive for most people, let alone college students living on a meager budget with the occasional spare change from the sofa tossed in. This chapter is a one stop shop for tips on how to not only eat well, but to eat cheap and to make your dollar stretch.

Hack #1: Stock your pantry with cheap, nonperishable, healthy foods.

Having a well-stocked pantry is going to be one of the best things you can do for your budget as a college student. Food can be expensive, and since it's a necessity, you can't really cross it off your list of monthly expenses like you can other things. Shopping for food doesn't have to all that hard on your wallet, though. Shopping smart is going to be the key silencing a hungry stomach and give your bank account a rest.

IN A NUTSHELL: Stock your pantry with cheap, non-perishable food. Then, supplement those staples with fresh or frozen vegetables and meat each week.

Why? Having a well-stocked pantry with healthy and cheap food options on hand is one of the best ways you can make your dollar stretch during those days when your bank account is a little on the lean side. Having a food budget and using it wisely is going to be a great way to put those Benjamin's to good use.

This is important because you'll need all the brain power you can muster to really apply yourself to your classes. Naturally, one of the best ways to ensure that happens is by eating healthy foods regularly. And there's a nice little bonus to this strategy, too: you'll stay fuller for longer, which means you may be able to hold off on grabbing a snack in between classes, which will also save you money.

The second reason to have a locked-and-loaded pantry with healthy, nonperishable treats is going to be the ease in which you can reach in for a snack. There will be times when you're short on time or up late cramming for a final and the siren song of the nearest fast food joint may be calling to you. If you're armed with food on hand, you can resist that impulse and nosh on some dried fruit instead. Talk about killing two birds with one stone! You'll get to eat some healthy food and save money. If that's not a winning combo then I'm not sure what is.

How? Ah, now we get into the good stuff! There are some really great and easy ways to get the most out of your money while walking away with a cart's worth of food.

For starters, make a list of cheap, non-perishable food to keep in your pantry. Luckily for you, if done that for you here! And remember, we're buying generic here. You're not going to be able to liveo n $15/day buying name-brand olive oil (that's almost $10 a bottle!). Anyway, check it out:

Cheap non-perishables + average cost:

- Brown rice ($1/b)
- Pasta ($2/lb)
- Wheat flour ($3/lb)
- Black beans ($1/lb)
- Kidney beans ($1/lb)
- Oats ($2/lb)
- Canned vegetables ($2/lb)
- Tuna ($3/lb)
- Olive oil ($5/16oz)

Excluding olive oil, those staple foods cost, on average, $1.87 *per pound of food*. If you spend just $20 (one week's food budget), you could get *almost 11 pounds of food*. Even if prices are higher where you live (not likely, since I'm in Chicago), and you can only buy nine pounds of food, that's insane. Obviously, that'd be a bit bland, so I don't recommend that. But in a pinch, you can certainly buy the calories you need.

Here are a just few dishes you can make with these ingredients, spices and a few veggies:

- Spaghetti
- Taco salad
- Stir fry
- Oatmeal
- Pancakes
- Lemon chicken
- Tuna salad
- Chicken and dumplings
- Lasagna

And here are my personal favorites, since you can make one huge batch and eat them throughout the week:

- Chili
- Vegetable soup
- Beef and bean stew
- Gumbo

And that's just the tip of the iceberg. There are *so many* ways you can combine those ingredients to really knock your dinners out of the park.

On a related note, it's important to know your likes and dislikes when it comes to your food choices. Try to be honest with yourself here, too, because it does you no good to stock up on foods that you don't like and that will just serve as dust collectors in your pantry. You can surely find other uses for the money you'd spend on foods that you'd only eat during a zombie apocalypse. Simple enough, right?

When you're out shopping, keep your eyes peeled for sales and markdowns. You'd be surprised at the awesome finds you can score if you're a vigilant shopper. Sure, you may not need 10 bags of black beans right at this moment, but finding a sweet deal may encourage you to stock up and save a few bucks.

Clipping coupons isn't just something your mom does anymore! Nope, get out the scissors and get to clipping, my friends. Make sure that you only clip coupons for the foods that you are actually going to eat and need to fill up your pantry. In other words, ignore the EasyMac coupons; pounce on the pasta coupons.

Lastly, a great way to fill your pantry with good, healthy foods at a cheap price is definitely to hit up your nearest warehouse super store to buy some of your most used items in bulk. Be careful here as well, though, as it's easy to fall into a similar trap to the one set by coupons. Before you add something to your cart, ask yourself if you really need six boxes of pasta or 30 pounds of rice. If you use those two staples in a lot of your meals, awesome, load up that cart and away you go! If you don't, move along to something else that you *do* like to eat.

Shortcut: The more organized you are, the easier and faster the process of food shopping is going to be. Create a nice little system for yourself so you are on top of things before you head to the store. Simple ways to keep organized are to clip and organize your coupons before you shop, keep a running list of items you've run out of so you don't forget and have to run out for something again and also take a look at the grocery store ads before you shop as well.

You'll get this process down to a science and the time you save can be directed towards studying or maybe even the mythical thing known as sleep that so many college students can only day dream about.

Bonus! Before you head out to the store, sit down and make a meal plan for the week (or longer if your shopping trips are spread out more). Once you've locked in your meals, take a look at what you've already got on hand and then make your final list to shop with. I know this sounds like unnecessary work, but trust me – it's worth it as you will save time and money and we all know that those are precious commodities to a college student.

Hack # 2 Try eating one large meal per day and a few small snacks to cut your grocery bill in half.

Skipping meals may not sound appealing, but lots of people have created an awesome 1-meal lifestyle. In addition to saving a bit of money, it can actually be really healthy to boot. This is a perfectly effective way to cut back on your grocery bill and still keep your stomach from rumbling in the library while studying.

IN A NUTSHELL: Eat one large, nutritious meal per day instead of three. Supplement that meal with a few small snacks and plenty of water.

Why? Cutting your meals down to one per day might sound like a totally nutty thing to do. But it's really not. In fact, a lot of people have adopted it as a way of life *purely for health reasons*.

This way of eat was largely introduced to the mainstream masses by a guy named Ori Hofmekler, who called it "The Warrior Diet."

He contends that our super-ancient ancestors ate this way for thousands of years because they had to. They would hunt and gather during the day, and they would eat what they caught at night.

Plus, there are plenty of scientifically backed benefits to fasting most of the day, including, among other things, a longer life span.

Of course, this isn't going to be the right meal plan for everyone, but it's a very good way to save money. If you're only eating one meal per day, you can essentially stock up on dinner (or breakfast or lunch) supplies. I personally like to eat my big meal at dinner, so I have a lot of pasta, rice and chicken. I might eat a piece of fruit or two during the day, drink plenty of water, and cook myself a nice, big, colorful, nutritious meal when I get home from work (or school, when I was a student).

How? The best way to implement a meal plan like this is to eat your big meal when it's most convenient for you to prepare something healthy and really filling. It won't do you much good if you toss together a lackluster meal that will only leave you hungry and in need of a full meal again later.

So, take a moment to determine when you are most likely to go to town on some food and while you're at it, go ahead and plan out your meals for the week! Keep in mind that this will be your only real meal each day, so load up on protein and other essentials to pack as much power into the meal as possible.

Next, you'll probably want to plan on 1-2 snacks on hand each day to keep the hunger pains at bay—at least to start. Fruit is usually the cheapest snack, since you can get a bag of apples for a few bucks. Eventually, though, you should be able to fast most of the day and feel really great.

Shortcut: I already mentioned a great shortcut by way of planning out your big meals for the week and that's still a great one to utilize. It will be nice to drop your books after a long day of learning and head right to cooking your meal. No guess work, no last minute store runs for a missing ingredient and no need to blow your budget on a pizza because you're too hungry to figure out a meal.

You can also prepare your snacks ahead of time for the week to save time and any last minute panic before heading out the door each day. All you have to do is grab your bag of snacks right after you grab your bag of books and you are good to go!

Bonus! Drink a lot of water when you're on this meal plan. Water is a great way to keep your body hydrated, and it's a great way to curb those hunger pains that are bound to pop up until your body adjusts to the new routine. Our bodies sometimes confuse hunger for dehydration, so chugging some water will help you see if it's snack time or if you just needed some aqua therapy.

You can carry a reusable water bottle around with you all day and refill as needed either at water fountains or in your dorm room. Using a reusable water bottle is cheaper than a case of water in plastic bottles and it's better for the environment.

Hack # 3: Cook in batches to save time and money.

Cooking your meals in batches is a really smart way to save on your food bill and cut down on the guesswork when the time comes to eat after a long day in class. There is something so effortless about grabbing a meal out of the freezer in the morning and having it thawed out by the time your ready to eat dinner. No muss and no fuss for this hack!

IN A NUTSHELL: Set aside one day a week, cook all your meals and freeze them. Then, just reheat to eat!

Why? Batch cooking saves you lots of money in the long run because it cuts down on ingredients, and it keeps you from eating out, which is about a million times more expensive than cooking for yourself.

It also saves a lot of time, and you can always turn that time into money (if you want) by pursuing a part-time job or starting some other profit-driven project. All it takes is a few hours of cooking one day out of your week or month (depending on how big your batches and freezer are), rather than the time it takes to prep, cook and clean up daily.

How? First, you'll need to sit down and decide what types of dishes you really like and will be able to eat frequently during the time amount of time you are cooking for. You can keep it simple and cook one big dish for the week or take it up a notch with a few different dishes to last you a few weeks to a month. Definitely keep in mind the ingredients needed and try to work around meals that have some of the same stuff so that you can save some money and cut down on extra cooking time.

Next, you'll need to make your list for the store and take a look at coupons or store ads for additional savings if possible. Also, make sure to take a peek in your pantry before finalizing your list since you may already have some of the ingredients on hand and it will save you from spending money on an unneeded item. You'll also want to make the initial investment in some freezer storage containers or baggies. Either option is fine, and the one you select will really just need to fit into your budget and freezer space. I know that this may be a bit tough if you're on a super tight budget, so I'll throw some tips and tricks at you in the bonus section in just a bit!

You're now ready to hit the store for your groceries! While you're shopping, keep your eyes peeled for any super steals and markdowns. You may find these in the produce and meat sections as those foods only have a limited shelf life, but that shouldn't be an issue for you since you're just going to go home and cook right away. When you're adding things to your cart don't be afraid to compare the prices of name brand items to store brand items either. Most of the big labels actually produce the products for the stores just with different labels, so don't be afraid to buy the cheaper items to stretch your budget. Hey, this may just be a way to squeeze in those freezer storage containers or bags too!

Once you've loaded up your cart and cracked open the piggy bank, it's time to go home and start chopping, dicing and sauteing! I prefer to work in an assembly line when I'm going in batches because it cuts down on the mess and ultimately the time spent slaving over a hot stove. You can cook all the ingredients that go into multiple dishes at once too, so that you've already got it ready to add to each one when the time comes.

When all the prepping and cooking is done, you can let the dishes cool for a while as you are cleaning up or taking a study break. I prefer to clean as I go so I'm not left with a mound of dishes and I can use the cool down time more efficiently, but that's just my style and you can certainly do whatever floats your boat. You'll definitely want to let everything get nice and cool before packaging it up in your containers or bags since that is the best way to keep the flavors intact and keep your meals from spoiling or from raising the temp of your freezer. Safety first because we don't want any stomach aches!

Lastly, you are going to divvy up your dishes into meal size portions and put them into your preferred freezer storage. Grab a permanent marker to write the date and dish down so that you know what you're eating and how fresh it is. Now pop those bad boys into the freezer and go about your business and rest easy knowing that your big meals are covered for a while. Hopefully you're also able to add some change back to your piggy bank because you saved a few clams at the store by scoping out some awesome deals.

Shortcut: One of the best shortcuts I can offer up here is to prepare as much as possible before you're ready to hit the store. You can have a list of recipes on hand to roll through to avoid getting into a food rut, check for deals and coupons ahead of time and maybe even work through your budget to ensure that the meals you'd like to make fit within it. I know that these don't seem like real shortcuts, but they really are and you'll be able to easily see how much smoother the process goes with these things out of the way early on.

Bonus! Ok, so we mentioned tips and tricks for the freezer storage options a while ago and we're ready to give up the goods on that now! A great little bonus tip for storage options is to get one of the machines that vacuum seals food because they will save you time and money in the long run. These machines can be a bit pricey, so adding these to your birthday or Christmas wish list is a good idea even if it's not the most exciting gift ever.

My next tip is for those of you that opt to go the freezer baggie route. This is a totally fine option, but those bags can get a bit pricey and who wants to shell out that kind of cash for something you're going to throw away, right? Wrong! Put out the money for the bags if your budget allows and if you are limited on space. You can reuse the baggies when you're done by washing them out really well and storing them for your next cooking marathon. You'll get some bang for your buck and be able to say you reduced your carbon footprint a bit. One last thing about freezer baggies before we move on...You can sometimes find coupons for baggies or even get them for super cheap at value stores, so check that option out too.

Hack #4: Make a list of the cheapest, healthiest foods and know which expensive to avoid.

Eating healthy doesn't have to be expensive. There are a lot of foods out there that are totally affordable, healthy and will make your meals stretch. Knowing what these foods are before stepping into the store is a great tool to have and use to save yourself some stress when it's time to check out.

We talked about this a bit a few chapters ago, but I wanted to give you a more detailed list of the cheapest health foods, so you can really start to wrangle your grocery list.

IN A NUTSHELL: Learn the foods that are healthy and affordable so you can shop smart. Keep a list and check that list against the most in-season foods to find the best deals, especially for produce.

Why? This is a great way to eat well without spending a fortune. When you know what to shop for within your budget, it will enable you to shop smarter and utilize the foods available to you in healthy, new ways. You'll also be able to dodge the more expensive items out there and substitute them for items that are more your speed financially

Remember, that you can find great, cheap foods that will produce the same healthy results that more pricey options do. You don't have to sacrifice taste, health benefits or affordability if you know what to shop for.

How? For starters, you'll want to do some research to find out if your favorite foods are on the list of affordable, healthy options or it they are on the list to avoid. If you've got a lot of favorites on the expensive list, try researching comparable substitutes that may jive with your affordable list. Hopefully a lot of your preferred foods will mainly fall under the cheap side of the list, though and you're not let scratching you head over what to eat.

Once you've completed your lists, hit the ads for your favorite grocery store and see if you can find more ways to save. You can implement this hack with the others in this chapter like creating a meal plan and finding recipes for your batch cooking sessions. You may be able to make your dollar stretch even further by swapping out some of the more expensive ingredients with some that are cheaper, which will make the overall value of your meals/recipes all the better.

I used this method during my own college years with only a tiny food budget to work with. I made a list of foods that were healthy and all under $2. You can buy frozen, fresh or a combo of the two as long as the price is right. Here are some of the cheap healthy foods I would shop for:

Vegetables

- Carrots
- Broccoli
- Green pepper
- Onion
- Cabbage
- Spinach
- Heads of lettuce

Protein

- Eggs
- Pork
- Chicken thighs
- Canned Tuna
- Legumes (beans, lentils and chickpeas)
- Sunflower seeds

Fruits

- Apples
- Bananas
- Oranges

Carbs

- Oats
- Sweet potatoes
- Brown rice
- Wheat pasta

Here is a list of some of the foods to stay away from since they are a bit on the expensive side and may have less health value per serving:

- Luxury cuts of meat, like t-bones (unless on sale)
- Avocados
- Grapes
- Fresh herbs (go for dried)
- Most nuts

I'm not telling you that you shouldn't ever buy any of the foods on the last list, but rather to do so with caution and when they are on sale.

Shortcut: Review the ads, clip the coupons and plan your meals according to what foods are on your list in order to save some money. I know this doesn't sound like a shortcut, but it is. You won't risk running out of food money and will spend less time searching for spare change or selling stuff on eBay.

Bonus! Again, don't be afraid to buy frozen fruits, veggies and even protein when you can. There's nothing wrong with frozen foods of this nature and they are often cheaper. You can also check out the farmers market for some good deals on foods that may only have a bit of shelf life left. This is a great way to squeeze the most you can out of your budget.

Clothing Hacks

Much like food, clothing is a necessity—and an expensive one at that. Clothing yourself doesn't always have to break the bank, though! The hacks offered up here will allow you to clothe yourself while on a budget and remain just stylish enough.

Hack #5: Never pay full-price for clothes and try to by good, high-quality brands.

You can't exactly walk around campus in your skivvies. There are work-arounds that will keep you clothed within your budget and this hack is a good place to start. I'm not saying that you have to go buy a bunch of designer duds by any means, though, as that is a one way ticket to the poor house!

IN A NUTSHELL: Instead of buying cheap clothes every season, troll thrift stores (and other places listed below) for ultra-durable, classic clothes by good brands that will last for years. You'll save tons of money in the long run.

Why? Clothing is an unavoidable expense and finding ways to afford the necessities can really seem like a daunting task when you don't have much cash to work with. This is where this hack will come in handy and save you money in the grand scheme of things.

When you buy (or find, or trade for) a few articles of clothing that you intend to use frequently made from better quality materials, you will get a lot more life out of them.

This is especially true with stuff you'll wear more than 2-3 times a week, like:

- Coats
- Jackets
- Jeans
- Shoes
- Boots
- Socks

The idea here is to buy great stuff—**as long as you're not paying full price for it**—so you won't have to replace it for a long time.

In the end, it's all about saving money and staying on a budget, which is totally doable once you fork over the initial investment on a few staple wardrobe pieces.

How? For starters, you'll want to take a look at your closet as it stand now and determine which articles of clothing you wear the most. This will help you decide what you want to spend more money on, since it will get the most use and is subject to more wear and tear.

Also, try to keep in mind that you won't be buying new clothes every season, so try to consider items that will suit your needs year round. For example, I bought about five high quality polo shirts and a couple high-quality button-up shirts. I can wear those in any season.

Once you've got an idea of what you wear the most, you'll need to think about how practical these clothing items are and if they will transition well from day to day. It's a great idea to opt for classic pieces that will work anywhere and for (almost) anything—stuff that won't go out of style in the near future. You don't want to drop the dough on a fad item that you won't want to be caught dead in next semester, so stick to the basics. If you don't know what that stuff is, just Google fashion icons, and look at the stuff people were wearing in the 1920s-1960s. If it still looks cool, it's classic. As a general rule, though, the best classic styles are simple and clean

Just because you're going to be shopping for the best clothes doesn't mean you want to pay the highest prices (of course). In fact, we strongly recommend you **never pay full price for clothes.** Ever.

There are just way too many places you can find good clothes for cheap or free, which will save you gobs of money. Here are just a few places you can look.

- Thrift stores (duh)
- Swap meets
- Friends and relatives

The idea is to find great brands for cheap or free. And really, if an article of clothing is free, the quality doesn't matter as much, since you're getting tons of value per dollar anyway.

Bonus! Hit up your local colleges' theater and fashion departments. Students in those classes make a discard clothes and costumes all the time, and they very often have stuff lying around that you can take home for almost nothing.

Many of these departments donate clothes anyway, so they'll usually be happy to send them home with someone who can use them.

Shortcut: The best shortcut here is to pay attention to your clothing habits and the condition of your most worn items. Once you've got that on lock, starting price hunting and snag the best deals possible for the more expensive staples needed to sustain your wardrobe.

Plan to buy clothes about once every three years, focusing on your most frequently worn items. That shouldn't be a problem if you're shopping for super high-quality clothes.

Hack #6: Learn to sew.

I'm not expecting you to pull a Julie Andrews and start making your clothes out of drapes or anything, but being skilled with a needle and thread will be rather handy during your college days. It won't be such a big deal when your jeans get a hole or your favorite sweater has a loose seam, if you know how to fix it.

IN A NUTSHELL: You can save hundreds of dollars if you patch things and alter your own clothes up instead of buying new clothes after every little rip and tear.

Why? Who wants to run to the tailor or have to toss your favorite shirt when it's got a hole or rip? Not me! Who has the money or the time for that? If you're a college student, I bet you're nodding in agreement right now. Save yourself the money and just fix it up on your own.

You don't need much to be your own personal tailor or seamstress and it won't cost a heap to get the supplies you need to do so. Some needles, thread, scissors and maybe an inexpensive sewing machine will do the job nicely. You'll save a ton from not having to replace clothes as often and by not having to pay someone else to do the fixing.

Another hash mark in the positive column, if you need another reason to pick up a thimble, is the ability to get creative and tweak your existing wardrobe. By doing this, you're creating something new that totally fits your style and you're recycling something that's just been hanging around waiting to be donated or tossed in the garbage.

How? The most basic sewing techniques are absurdly easy, and you can almost certainly figure it out on your own. But, in a nutshell, this is how to repair a small rip in your clothes:

1. Thread the needle with about double the thread you need
2. The thread should pass through the needle, and the ends should meet at the bottom
3. So the thread will actually be *two* threads
4. Tie a small knot at the end
5. Pass the needle and thread through both sides of the rip until the knot at the end stops the thread
6. Loop the thread around and pass it through the same side
7. Continue for the length of the rip
8. When you're finished, loop the needle under the last stitch and tie it off
9. Presto! Finished.

Of course, if you want to do something more complicated, like altering your clothes to fit you if you gain or lose weight, you'll have to do a bit of research (this isn't a sewing book after all!).

There are tons of resources available on the internet to help you learn how to sew and mend your clothing. You can watch YouTube videos, read tutorials, cruise Pinterest or study diagrams. There's pretty much a tip or trick for any learning style out there, so hit Google first to see what you can find.

If learning a new skill from the Web isn't really your speed, no worries! You can always ask your friends for help, pointers and to demonstrate how to get the job done. It may be pretty helpful to hear and see the way things are done in person with the ability to interject your questions as they come up. You can also see the supplies your friends have and find out where they got them and for how much.

If you strike out on the internet or are lacking friends that can wield a needle, you can always call your dear old Mom for some pointers. Sure, you may have to endure stories about how she used to sew your baby clothes out of old t-shirts, but a trip down memory lane is worth saving some money and revamping some old clothes.

Shortcut: The only real shortcuts available here are to already have a little stash of sewing supplies on hand and to learn how to use them to fix up your clothes before you have a problem. This will at least save you a trip to the store and from having to learn a new skill when your favorite pair of jeans has a broken zipper.

Bonus! It's a pretty good idea to check out your local craft store for sewing classes since they are often free or relatively inexpensive. You can get hands-on training from people that really know what they are doing, and they may even be able to show you some cool tricks that you can use when you're re-purposing an old garment.

You can also keep your eyes open for coupons for craft stores in the paper or on the internet. This is a great way to save money on some of the sewing essentials and may even allow you a bit of wiggle room to get extra goodies to spruce up your old duds. In any case, though, a spool of thread is always going to be cheaper than a new pair of jeans.

One more bonus or you fashion forward sewers-to-be: check out Pinterest or other online forums for ideas, tutorials and tips when and if you decide to liven up those old shorts or add a new standout trim to your favorite skirt.

Hack #7: Organize clothing swaps.

Clothing swaps aren't just for neighborhood churches anymore, my friends! College students all over are getting in on the swap action to pass around old clothes and pick up some new ones. You never know what you can find at events like this and it's a great way to keep within your budget when you get bored with your wardrobe.

IN A NUTSHELL: If you need clothes, trade for them instead of buying them. The best way to do this is usually by organizing a clothing swap.

Why? Buying durable clothes and learning to sew is a great starting point, but sometimes you just need some new clothes. When that happens, you can sometimes get them 100% for free if you just trade your old clothes with your friends.

Organizing a swap meets both of these needs without requiring you to dip into your bank account when you don't have the extra to spend.

Organizing a clothing swap is also a great way to purge your closet of unwanted clothes that are too small, too big or that you just don't like. You can pass them on to someone else and replace them with items that will hopefully get more use.

How? For starters, go through your closet and drawers! Take anything and everything out that hasn't been worn in the last six months and anything that doesn't fit or you just don't like anymore. This goes for your shoes too! While they may still fit you, you may not wear them anymore and you might as well get something new out instead.

Once you've got your clothes sorted and organized, pick a date, find a space to hold the swap and set up some guidelines to avoid any issues and to ensure that all swaps are fair for both parties. After you've locked in all the details, start reaching out to your friends and classmates. Encourage them to do the same so that there is a good variety of clothing to swap around when the time comes.

As the swap approaches, touch base with everyone that intends to participate and make sure that all times, locations and rules are solidly in place. It won't be much fun to have confusion and chaos on the day of the swap, so it's best to cover all the bases beforehand to avoid any hiccups.

You're pretty much ready to start swapping clothes at this point and begin the process of sprucing up your closet! Keep in mind the space you have available to store your new duds and what items you may need to fill in any gaps in your wardrobe.

Shortcut: A great shortcut here is to go through your closet every few months to purge and organize it. You'll be able to accumulate a good supply for the swaps, see what you have, see what you need and keep yourself organized. Doing this on a regular basis will make the pre-swap purge less of a chore because you'll be on top of the process already. The whole process will be much more enjoyable this way, trust me.

Bonus! Organizing a purge is really pretty easy on a college campus and can be easily be done from your dorm room. If you'd like to take the "go big or go home" approach, you can do that with relative ease well. Creating a Facebook event is a great way to let everyone know when and where the purge is going to be held. You can also put notices on bulletin board around campus and in the common room of dorms.

Housing Hacks

By now, most of you have spread your wings and left the safe nest of your parents' house. This new found independence comes along with some hefty housing expenses and no one to shoulder those burdens but you. This is an area that is particularly important when it comes to inventive ways to save, so read closely and implement anything you can.

Hack #8: Split the rent as many ways as possible, even if you have to share a room.

I know that sharing yours space with someone isn't likely to be something you are super excited about. It can cramp your living style a bit and cut down on the privacy you may be used to, but the cash it will save you in rent and utilities alone is worth being able to run around in your skivvies if that's your usual Friday night fun.

IN A NUTSHELL: Find enough roommates to spit the rent more ways than there are rooms (i.e. split it four ways if there are two rooms) to drastically reduce your rent.

Why? Well, the main reason to shack up with a roommate is to ease the financial burden that comes with living on your own. Housing isn't cheap, and it can be super stressful to manage a big monthly expense like rent. It's enough to make anyone feel the financial pressure.

Having enough roommates to split the rent of each bedroom is one of the best ways to take a major chunk out of your financial obligations.

Here's some simple math for you. Suppose you found a reasonably nice 2-bedroom apartment with decent living space close to your school and/or work. The rent for this pad is $1,000 and the utilities come out to about $170 each month. Renting it alone would obviously be a disaster.

But what if you had three roommates, and you shared one of those rooms?

Your rent would go from $1,000 per month to $250, and your utility bill would go from $170 per month to $42.50.

That's a 75% decrease in all monthly expenses.

How? Find a friend (or two) who is in the market to save some money on housing, is financially stable enough to contribute to the household equally and who you don't mind running into on your way to the bathroom at 2 A.M.

For starters, I suggest putting pen to paper with a good old pros and cons list. If you're going to sign a lease with someone, you're going to want to make sure you've considered all the possibilities and are making an informed decision. Here are some of the things I added to my list when I was looking for a roommate:

- The potential to build a new and valuable friendship
- The potential to ruin an old and valuable friendship
- Cheaper rent and utilities
- Less privacy
- Sharing household responsibilities
- Possibly butting heads of sharing household responsibilities
- Do you feel safe and comfortable around the potential roommate?

Once you've made your list and checked it twice, you can decide if having a roommate is for you. If so, then open up the dialogue about a potential living arrangement pronto so you can iron out the details.

Find some time to sit down with your new roomie to discuss their financial situation to make sure that you're both on the same page. Nothing will ruin this experience more than finding out that your new roommate can't uphold their end of the deal after you've already committed to a lease. Ask some general questions about how they view their money, how much they make and even toss in some questions about careers goals. This should give you info to decide if you're going to jive financially.

You're obviously going to need a place to live, so start searching for a place that meets your space needs, is within your budget and is not crazy far away from school/work. You may not agree on every little detail, but that's ok as long as the important ones are covered.

You'll want to iron out the details of the lease in terms of who is on it and who is not. If only one of you is signing on the dotted line, then draft up a roommate agreement that covers all the basis and get that bad boy signed. It protects everyone involved and makes things clear cut if anything should come up.

If you haven't discussed how expenses are going to be divided up by now, have your new roommate smack you because this is an important detail. If you're using equal space, split everything straight down the middle to make it easy. You can work out the details of where the money for bills goes and whose name said bills are in as well. Make it fair and easy to avoid any confusion when the due dates roll around.

For any extra additions like cable, phone or the internet, make sure to check in with your roommate before assuming these things are wanted and can be afforded. If your bunkmate isn't on board, you'll have to shoulder those payments alone and may want to think about a sharing agreement or something if they will be used by others.

Food is often a point of contention among roommates as can be expected when you reach in the fridge to grab the new container of milk and find the empty carton instead. It's probably safest to just eat what you buy and chip in extra for times when you eat together. No one gets made that way and no one goes hungry.

Shortcut: There aren't many ways to shortcut this process other than moving someone into you're current dwelling and picking a roommate that you've already established a good roommate track record with. Other than that, you'll have to take the long route to get the job done.

Bonus! This can be a lot easier if you (1) split a room with your significant other or (2) find a couple to be your roommates. There tend to be much fewer disagreements when couples share a room than friends (and I shouldn't have to tell you why). So, if you can get a couple on board with your plans, that's probably the best route.

Hack #9: If you're going to college for 4 years, check to see if it's cheaper to rent or buy.

In some housing markets, it can actually be cheaper to buy than to rent. This book isn't necessarily a long-term investment guide, but it pays to remember that if you do buy instead of rent, you get all your money back when you sell the house; when you rent, it's gone forever.

IN A NUTSHELL: Check the housing market in your area. If the mortgage payment on a house is cheaper than a similarly sized apartment, consider joining forces with 4-5 responsible friends to buy a house instead of renting an apartment.

Why? Did you know that you can buy a house with a mortgage payment that is less than some rent payments? Yep, you totally can.

It's not the case in all markets, but it's certainly the case in some. For example, in my Chicago neighborhood, mortgage payments can be as low as 40% of the rent of a similarly sized apartment. That's nuts!

If you can swing a good mortgage, you'll pay less for a space you own, which means your monthly living expenses will decrease a lot when you divide everything up among your roommates.

You can find some really sweet deals out there on houses and can potentially fatten your return when you're ready to sell in four years. So, the potential to bank a nice chunk of change is definitely there if the market is right when you sell and if you find the time to make improvements along the way. Not a bad deal here, huh?

Becoming a home owner will also allow you to build some solid credit history, and we all know how important having good credit is these days. Having an established line of credit can help you get a new car, more student loans if you need them (hopefully you don't) and can even help you land a good job after college. Think of it as laying the foundation for a brighter future.

How? The very first thing you need to do when buying a house is to take a good hard look at your credit as it stands right now. You can do this by pulling your credit report from the three credit bureaus offering free yearly credit reports without any fine print that will sign you up for a not so free service one the trial period ends. You can get your free reports from Equifax, Experian and TransUnion online with minimal effort.

Make sure your credit reports look accurate and on the up and up. If you question anything, don't hesitate to contact the reporting agencies for clarification and to clear up anything on your end. If you already have credit cards in your name, try to hold off on canceling them as it will actually lower your credit score. The amount you're granted for a loan may decreases as a result, so just leave them open and paid off if at all possible.

Once you're credit is in a good spot you can start gathering all of the paperwork needed to apply for a loan. When submitting an application to a lender, you'll need the following documents to get the job done:

- Tax returns dating back two years
- W-2 or 1099's from employers or clients
- Paycheck stubs from your last two checks
- Checking and savings account statements that are recent
- Credit card statements
- Car loan documentation

I know this sounds like a lot of stuff to gather, but it's really important for the lender to get a clear picture of what your financial situation is. This will ensure that you don't get approved for too much and bite off more of a mortgage payment than you and your roommates can chew. A reasonable down payment and monthly mortgage principal, interest, property taxes and insurance will also be calculated with this information to complete the big picture.

Next up, you'll have to come up with a budget that is reasonable and sustainable. Take it easy here and don't get too sidetracked by any figures thrown at you by the lender. **You don't have to buy a house that costs $150,000 just because that is the amount you qualified for.**

Stick to a budget that you and your roommates are comfortable with and that won't bleed you dry if some unforeseen shift in the living arrangement occurs.

Once all the not-so-fun financial stuff is out of the way, you can begin the search for your new house! This is an exciting and exhausting task, so work together with your friends to pick a place that is affordable, in an area that works for everyone, accommodates everyone in terms of space and isn't going to require a ton of extra work or money to become habitable.

When all the paperwork is signed, draft up the necessary documents to protect yourself and your roommates. Make sure that everyone is clear on the details of what monetary contributions are expected each month as well as what happens when the time to sell come along. This means making sure that everyone gets their cut when the house is sold after graduation.

Shortcut: If you know this is the route you want to go, start saving early on. Having some money for a down payment in a savings account incurring interest will get you going in the right direction. Plus, if you put some money down, you'll lower you monthly payments.

Bonus! Do yourself a favor and work with a realtor. Make sure that he/she knows your budget, where you want to live and how much space you need/want. Make sure that they take a look at foreclosures, short sales and fixer-uppers requiring minimal work. You can often find amazing prices in these areas and don't want to miss out on something because all bases weren't covered.

Maintenance is a part of being a homeowner, and it's not always cheap. Remember that you won't have a landlord to call on when something breaks, pest control is needed or when the yard needs to be tended to. It's all on you and your roommates now. So, keep on top of things and work together to take care of your home and all its working parts. It will save you from having to fork over a ton of money and will probably sweeten your payout when you sell.

Lastly...

I just want to stress that this isn't always the best decision. Buying a house is a major commitment, and it's certainly not worth it if the savings would only be $50 per month. That said, in some markets, buying instead of renting can give you a gigantic advantage and significantly lower your monthly expenses.

Hack #10: Pick a location close to school/work, even if it's a bit more expensive. Then, ditch your car.

There's nothing better than living in a central location that keeps you close to the places you go to the most like work and school. It makes it easy to get to where you need to go and quickly, which is especially helpful when you didn't hear your alarm and are late for your morning lecture. Sure, sometimes these areas can increase the price of housing, but the other ways you can save pretty much level the playing field.

IN A NUTSHELL: Find a house or apartment that is located within a reasonable distance from work or school. This cuts down own a lot of the extra expenses that incur when you have to travel long distances and will make your life a whole lot easier when life throws you a curve ball.

Why? Gas is expensive as is public transportation. Who wants to spend money on those things when you can bank it and walk or bike to work/school?

You can save a good $20 to $50 a week on these things (if not more) when you only have to drive a short distance or can walk/ride a bike. All of your savings will really add up too! Even if you only saved $20 a week on gas or public transportation, you'd have an extra $1040 a year. **That's equal to your entire food budget!**

Where there is a car, car trouble is bound to follow. No matter how much you baby your car, you can't predict when something is going to go wrong and it's probably going to happen at the worst time. You can thank Murphy and his stupid law for that!

Car trouble becomes less of an issue when you live close to work and school, though. You don't have to worry about missing work or class if you can just walk or ride a bike. No loss of pay or slipping grades here, my friends. Plus, you're saving money on gas while your car collects dust and waits for repairs.

So, pick a great location that is close enough to both your work and your school that you can either walk or bike for the next few years. Then, sell your car. If your car's in decent shape, you could get a few thousand dollars, which, for us, makes up a really big chunk of our yearly budget.

How? Do your research and try to find a new pad close to the two main places you spend the most time. You can use a realtor, the internet or pound the pavement in the hopes of spotting a for rent/sale sign. Check bulletin boards at school, work, the gym and even your local coffee shop. There may be the perfect place for you hanging out on a scrap piece of paper just waiting for you.

Ask around school and work for suggestions from your peers/co-workers. They may have heard of available units nearby and can point you in the right direction. Some of these folks may live nearby, but intend to move in the near future and can get you on the list to fill their spot. It certainly can't hurt to ask around and let people know you're looking. It may be just the thing needed to help you relocate and ditch your car.

Shortcut: You can try to make living close to work/school your goal right out of the gate as a way to start saving fast. Skip looking at places too far away and hone in on those nearby instead. If you come up empty handed then expand your search a bit until you find a place.

Bonus! If living close to your work or school isn't in the cards, no worries! You can always try to find a place near your favorite grocery store. You'll still save a bit of money with the convenience of being able to drive a short distance or walk/ride when you need to get some food. The savings won't be as big as they would be if you lived close work/school, but any savings is better than no savings in my book.

Hack #11: Go without a phone. Seriously!

I put this hack in the housing section because most people treat their phone bill like a necessary utility. But man. $100 is crazy if you're trying to live on the cheap! I'm being serious here. I really am suggesting you cut the cord and ditch your beloved cell phone. You'll be picking up what I'm dropping in no time, though. As soon as the weight of your phone in your palm is replaced by the cold hard cash you saved, you'll see the beauty in what I'm suggesting.

IN A NUTSHELL: You don't really NEED to have a phone to communicate with the world around you anymore. Instead of remaining a slave to big phone companies, it's time to drop the extra expense and switch to one of the other options out there. You can stay connected for cheaper, so why not give it a try?

Why? The rates associated with having a phone are slowing creeping up to the ridiculous zone, but most of us are unsure of what to do without a phone and continue to cover the bill each month. Times are changing and it's time to let go of the old, expensive way of doing things while sparing your piggy bank of the monthly hold up. Give some of the free voice services a try instead and save a couple of bucks.

Trying alternative means of communication will also release you from the contract chains that mobile carriers are so eager to bind you with. You don't have to worry about finding a way to afford the rest of a contract when finances are tight or if your phone kicks the bucket. There's no stress over the hefty fees associated with terminating a contract early or scrambling to afford a new phone. Kiss those concerns goodbye and move on to the next communication chapter!

How? Give Google Voice a try for starters. This nifty service is available to anyone living within the United States and is free in most cases. All you need is an email address, computer and a phone to make/receive calls from. No more data plan, text message fees or contracts to worry about. You can use Google Voice from home or on the go if need be. It's easy to use and will save you a ton, especially if you're torn between having a cell phone and land line.

Skype is still alive and kicking if you're not too sure about Google Voice. You can call land lines and cell phones for a super low monthly rate or pay as you go without the risk of your minutes expiring. All you need is a computer, tablet or phone with the ability to use data or a WiFi connection. Sure, you need to be connected to the internet somehow, someway to use it, but that's not really a huge issue when you consider how easy it has become to tap into a free wireless network. There is even a convenient little messaging option if you'd like to skip the added cost of text messaging here too. Skype is easy, cheap and pretty convenient.

Both Google Voice and Skype will help you stay connected through voice, text and even voicemail. You can still call your mom each Sunday to tell her when you'll be dropping your laundry off or text your lab partner to schedule a study session. Not much changes when using these voice services, except that you no longer have to cry over a monthly phone bill.

Shortcut: Weigh all your phone replacement options before you decide to torch your monthly plan. Make a pros and cons list for each voice option you're considering so that you can really figure out what's going to work best for you. It's better to find the best fit to avoid a relapse into the expensive abyss of phone contracts and bills.

You can also give each service a trial run if you can't decide which one is going to keep you connected. There aren't any contracts, so there's no harm in experimenting if that's more your speed. Just make the commitment to cutting out the phone and adding to your savings instead.

Bonus! If you're really resistant to change and insist on having a phone, there are options out there for you and at a good price. You can try Ting instead of any of the major carriers out there. Ting has super low rates that jive with your phone use rather than paying for minutes, data or texts that you don't use. They even allow you to bring your own device if you want and of course have new ones to choose from if you're not in possession of a compatible one. This is a really cool company with a real drive to make mobile communication available and affordable to everyone. They're changing the way things are done and your bank account will surely thank them.

Transportation Hacks

Whether you own a car or not, everyone can use some tips on how to safe on the cost of transportation, even if it's of the public variety. You're sure to save some cash if you give a few of these hacks a try.

Hack #13: Bike or walk whenever you can.

Your feet were made for walking, so put on some comfortable shoes and get to stepping. If walking isn't your favorite form of transportation, then dust off your Huffy and inflate those tires in an attempt to give Lance Armstrong a steroid-free run for his money! There's not much need for a car if you can get around easily and by cheaper means. Not to mention the brownie points you'll score for electing to reduce your carbon footprint.

Just remember, this won't be possible if you haven't nailed down Hack #10, since they're practically related. Well, really, they're the same thing, but we wanted to cover this one in a bit more detail.

IN A NUTSHELL: Ditch your car. Walk, bike or run instead.

Why? These are obviously very cheap means of transportation. The cost of walking is nonexistent and all you need is a good pair of shoes and some water on hot days. Riding a bike doesn't require much after the initial investment and maintenance costs are low since bike tires and chains aren't going to break the bank. You'll probably even have enough left over for one of those awesome bells if you play your cards right.

Cars are bad news for the environment with all of their emissions and use of fossil fuels. You can cross all three of these things off the list when you opt out of driving a car and use your own body to get around instead. You're contributing to the greater good of our planet and saving money on those planet damaging fossil fuels.

If I haven't sold you on ditching the four wheels yet, these next three little reasons will have you posting for sale ads in no time. You know what's great about not driving a car? Not having to pay a monthly car insurance payment. Want to know two benefits to ditching your car for bipedal locomotion? Not having to wait in traffic or find a place to park.

As with many things, the motivation to change our habits lies not within the reason, but rather in the dollar signs. So, here is an example of what you can save by walking or riding everywhere:

- Cost per mile for a bike: $0.10
- Cost per mile for a car: $0.62
- Average cost of owning and operating a bike per year: $308
- Average cost of owning and operating a car per year: $8,220

So, as you can clearly see, riding a bike is definitely going to save you a pretty penny and still allows you to get where you need to go.

How? When purchasing a bike, shop around for good prices and for one that fits your riding style. You can hit up bike shops for advice and to view their selections if you want a higher end bike. If you're not too concerned with bells, whistles and super comfy seats, you can always check out the selection at of bikes at your local big box retailer.

Shortcut: If you had a bike at home before heading off to college, bring it back with you after a trip home for mom to do your laundry. You won't have to spend more money on something that you already have and you can get some clean underwear.

Bonus! Check out garage sales, thrift shops and used sporting goods stores for a bike with a low price tag. You may need to replace the tires, chains and maybe even get a new seat, but that's likely to be doable if the price is right.

DIY Hacks

The budget of a college student doesn't always make the added expenses of repairs, household cleaners, nice furniture or quick fix health remedies, all that easy to afford. This chapter offers up just the right tips and tricks to get things fixed, clean, looking spiffy and feeling great again.

Hack #14: Learn to fix the 5 most commonly broken household things.

We've all been there...Something around the house breaks and at the worst time. If you rent, you may get lucky and have the issue taken care of by your landlord. For those of you that run into an issue that isn't covered on your lease or if you own your house, this is the hack for you!

IN A NUTSHELL: Cut out the middle man or in this case the repairman for most household maintenance needs. There is a lot of stuff you can fix yourself to safe money and time. It's also pretty awesome to be able to say "Yeah, it was broken, but I fixed it!"

Why? For starters and possibly most importantly, fixing things around your house or apartment on your own is going to save you a nice chunk of change in most cases...as long as you know what you're doing. You won't have to call a repair man to come out and pay him by the hour to take his sweet time fixing something that you could actually do yourself and much quicker. We'll get into the *what* and *how* of things to fix a bit later, so keep your eyes peeled for that info.

Another reason to strap on the tool belt is because it's great to have these skills up your sleeve and ready to use. Being self-sufficient and taking care of business is so valuable. It doesn't matter if you're a male or female either. Simply having the ability to fix things around the house is going to be a lifelong tool to use and has no expiration date.

How? You'll first want to research some of the most common things around the house that break and read up on how to fix them should something go wrong. The best place to read up on what to fix and how to do it, is definitely going to be on the internet since there is a ton of information available and you're more likely to find current threads pertaining to your issue. Start a special bookmarks folder for your finds and cut down on your search time when/if you need to put the information found to use.

So, what are some things you can fix on your own and how? Let's get into that right now!

Washing machines. Washing machines are responsible for a ton of household damage each year a due to cracked, busted, loose or leaky hoses. You don't have to call an appliance repair service to come out and fix this issue though! Check your hoses at the coupling spot and connection point to start. These are the two most common areas to experience an issue. If you notice anything out of the ordinary or if the hoses have been around for more than five years, it's time to replace them. Bypass the rubber hoses and replace the old ones with the braided stainless steel type. They are pretty affordable, easy to switch out and can save you from have a flood on your hands.

Dryers. Have you ever turned on your dryer and heard it rumble along as usual, only to open it later with clothes just as wet as when you put them in? Yeah, it's no fun; trust me. A lot of people would think that they need to call someone to come give it a once over or that a new dryer needs to be bought. Most of the time, neither of these things is needed. Nine times out of ten, the culprit is either too much lint in the lint trap or a worn out heating element. If it's lint, just clean it out by hand. For heating elements, you can buy a replacement for a pretty decent amount online since the ones available at appliance stores are usually double the price (this is the kind of thing your emergency budget is meant for). All you need to switch the elements out is a pair of pliers, a Philips head screwdriver and about 10 minutes of your time. You can find easy-to-follow videos on YouTube to help you get started. You'll have warm, dry clothes again in no time.

Plumbing issues. One of the most common and most dreaded household issues comes in the form of plumbing issues. Your drains and toilets are going to get clogged, but not every stubborn issues requires calling a licensed plumber to fix it. For stubborn clogs that you can't seem to break up, hot water is going to be your best friend. If you have metal pipes, use a tea kettle of boiling water to get things moving along and if you've got PVC pipes or unsure, go for super-hot tap water instead to avoid melting issues.

You likely have a plunger hanging around and can use that for your sinks, tubs/showers and toilets. Instead of plunging the old school way, apply some duct tape around the base to create a strong seal. If you're plunger-less, no problem. You can use an empty milk carton instead for small drain obstructions. Simply place the open end of the carton over the drain and squeeze the air into the drain. Viola! You now have a clear drain and saved a couple of bucks.

Simple wall repair. Walls take a beating whether it's from hanging things on the walls or the accidental hole in the drywall that was a result of a really intense game of ping-pong. No need to panic or spend money on having someone else fix it for you. For bigger holes, you'll need to hit the home improvement store for some inexpensive supplies like fiberglass tape, joint compound, sandpaper and a bit of paint. If you've got minor nail holes and flaws to cover up, a dab of caulk or spackling applied with your finger and a touch of pain will do the job.

Refrigerators. Not much is worse than a refrigerator that goes out when you've just stocked up on food. Not only are you possibly out of all the money for your food, but you're also looking at a hefty bill to get the fridge repaired or worse having to buy a new one. Before you get too upset and try to eat all the food before it goes bad, check the coils. This is the issue in over half of the service calls received by service pros and it's a super simple issue to fix.

The coils easily get dirty, especially if you've got pets as their hair likes to find its way to the wire and tubing grid. This will cause the grid to overheat the compressor and trigger the overload switch. Open the grill in the front or back of your fridge and use a coil cleaning brush to give them a good cleaning. Make sure you use a vacuum attachment to get the extra debris out too since you're already in there. Once the coils are cleaned up, they will cool down in a few hours and the overload switch will reset itself and turn the fridge back on. You'll have saved a pretty penny by fixing your own issue and you'll save a couple of bucks each month on your electric bill now that your unit doesn't have to work as hard.

Shortcut: The best way to avoid having major issues around the house is to keep up on the maintenance needed. When you first move in, give everything a good inspection and perform any repairs or cleaning needed early on. This will enable you to know the current state of things and may stave off problems. You can also set up your own maintenance schedule where you repeat this process and head off bigger problems.

Bonus! There's no denying the expensive nature of home repairs, but there are a few quick and cheap substitutes available when your piggy bank is feeling a little light. Try these things in a repair pinch:

- Use white-out in place of paint to cover small nail or tack holes in your walls. It's cheap and easy to find in a hurry.
- If you need to snake your drain because of a clog, use a plastic water bottle instead of buying one from the store.
- Use food coloring to find a toilet leak. Simply open the toilet lid, give it a flush and let it fill. Once the tank is filled up again, drip four to five drops of blue or red food coloring in and replace the lid. Find something to do for about 20 to 30 minutes and then check out the water in the toilet bowl. If it's clear, you're leak free. If it's tinted from the food coloring, you've got a leak and can begin researching the next step.

Hack #15: DIY these 5 household cleaners.

Having a clean house is great, but spending a ton of money on cleaning supplies to get it that way is not. You no longer have to break the bank to get your pad sparkling just like Mr. Clean's head anymore, though. Cut out the expensive products and make your own to save some money.

IN A NUTSHELL: Skip the cleaning isle at the store from now on by making your own household cleaners. You only need a handful of supplies to make different cleaners and you can use the same supplies for other things to get the most bang for your buck.

Why? It's all about the Benjamin's and how to save as many as possible. Making your own cleaning supplies is a really great way to stretch your money. Not only are the ingredients inexpensive, but they are able to be used for other things. You're killing two birds with one very clean stone.

Mass-produced cleaners have a lot of chemicals in them that aren't exactly the best for use to be exposed to and they can be harmful to the environment. You'll know every single component of the cleaners you make, so you'll rest easy knowing that you're not exposing yourself, anyone else or the planet to harsh additives.

You'll even save some time by making your own cleaners. Gone are the days of running to the store when you run out of glass cleaner, floor cleaner or laundry soap. You can easily whip these things up in a hurry or even make them in batches to refill when you get low. This way you'll save a trip to the store, save gas and have more time to study.

How? There are five types of cleaners that are most frequently used by households and they are: all purpose cleaner, glass cleaner, floor cleaner, laundry soap and bathroom cleaner. All five of these DIY cleaners can be made with 10 simple, cheap and environmentally friendly ingredients too. You'll need the following supplies to get started:

- White vinegar
- Baking soda
- Lemons and/or lemon juice
- Salt
- Olive Oil
- Ivory bar soap
- Liquid dishwashing soap
- Washing soda
- Borax powder
- Essential oils (I prefer to use lemon, orange and lemongrass for most cleaners. Thieves is a great oil for your all-purpose cleaner due to its anti-bacterial properties)

You'll want to have empty spray bottles and containers with lids around too. These things are pretty inexpensive and can be used for a long time.

Here's are a few of the quick and easy cleaner recipes that you can whip up before your next cleaning binge!

All Purpose Cleaning Spray:
Ingredients:
1 tablespoon borax

1 tablespoon washing soda
1 teaspoon dishwashing soap
1 cup white vinegar
4 cups hot water
25-30 drops essential oil (optional, but it makes it smell great)

All you have to do is add all of the ingredients together in a big bowl and give it a good whisk for about a minute. Pop a funnel into the neck of your spray bottle and pour it in. You will use it just like any store bought cleaner and come away with a clean, disinfected area.

Glass Cleaner:
Ingredients:
1 ½ cups vinegar
1 ½ cups water
5-10 drops essential oil (optional)

Pour water and vinegar into a spray bottle followed by essential oil if you use it then give it a vigorous shake. You're ready to start cleaning your windows! I like to use a squeegee or old crumpled newspaper instead of rags or paper towels. You get less streaks and lint that way.

Laundry Detergent:
Ingredients:
1 bar Ivory soap
1 cup borax
1 cup washing powder

Grab a microwave safe bowl and toss in the Ivory soap bar, pop the bowl in the microwave for about 2 minutes or until you see the soap turn into a foam. Take your bowl of foamy soap and start stirring it quickly to break it up into little soap chips. Add in the borax and washing powder while you continue to mix. You've now made laundry detergent! Give the detergent a bit of time to cool down to room temperature and then transfer it to a container with an airtight lid. A little bit of this goes a long way, so you will only need to use 1-2 tablespoons for each load. Your best bet is to use it with warm or hot water washes. If you'd rather stick with a cold wash routine, go ahead and dissolve the detergent in about ¼ cup hot water before adding it to your washer.

Shortcut: I like to make batches of these DIY cleaners that will last me a few months at a time. I never run out this way and save time by getting it all done in one shot. Set a reminder on your phone or pencil it into your calendar. You can also jot down any supplies you need to replenish ahead of time to avoid a last minute run to the store.

Bonus! You can save a bit of extra money by also making your own reusable cleaning accessories. Things like "unpaper towels" and reusable sponges, are simple and cheap to make along with being really effective cleaning tools. You can use them and toss them in the wash instead of having to throw them away and buy new like you do with other items.

Hack #16: Make your own simple furniture using reclaimed stuff.

Money is tight when you're in college and there will be times when you have to make something out of nothing as a result. You can still have nice furniture that is unique with a pretty cool story behind it, even if you did make it out of wooden crates and plywood.

IN A NUTSHELL: Make your own furniture out of items that seem to lack purpose and turn them into something awesome with a few tools, imagination and sweat. Furnish your pad on a budget with simple, functional pieces instead of spending a bunch of money at IKEA.

Why? Making something out of nothing with your own two hands can be a rewarding experience and a valuable new skill to have. It doesn't take much more than some tools and the ability to read directions to make cool furniture. You'll have full creative control to make whatever you want out of whatever you can.

Investing in some good furniture building tools is a whole lot less costly than having to buy furniture. You don't need to buy out the whole tool store to get going and they will surely get used when you realize how easy making your own stuff is. These are a few tools I suggest filling your tool box with if you start building your own furniture:

- Drill/Driver
- Claw Hammer
- Screwdrivers of varying heads and sizes
- Pliers
- Levels in small, medium and large
- Tape Measure
- Handsaw
- Staple Gun

If you plan to really get into making furniture and embark on big project, you may want to break out the big guns with these tools:
- Power sander
- Nail gun
- Compound miter saw
- Table saw or circular saw

How? Think about some furniture that you want or need and then hit the internet for some easy to follow tutorials. Keep in mind that you can use items you already have around the house or things that you can pick up for cheap. You'll want to start out with simple projects to avoid biting off more than you can chew, so consider a few of these as starter projects:
- Turn an old grocery store pallet into a bookshelf
- Make wall shelves with old wooden planks
- Turn picket fence sections into picture frames

You won't need any fancy tools to complete these projects and they can be further enhanced with some fun paint, fabric or furniture stain. Once you've constructed the pieces, let your creativity run wild.

When you've mastered some starter projects, you can expand your horizons and tool collection with bigger pieces of furniture. You can still make simple items and keep your supply costs low with bigger projects too. Give one of these a whirl when you're ready:

- Build a coffee table out of wooden crates
- Use an old spare tire as the structure for a new ottoman
- Construct a dinner table out of wood planks of various sizes

You'll need some more advanced tools to complete projects of this size, so be sure that you're really invested in the process before you spend the money. There's not much sense in buying them if you're not going to follow through and let the tools collect dust.

Shortcut: Be on the lookout for items that can be reclaimed and made into something new. Don't be afraid to grab something left on the curb if it looks like it has potential. You'll save some money this way and time by having the bones of a new furniture piece on hand when inspiration strikes.

Bonus! Become a regular at thrift stores and consignment shops. You'll be able to find some great items that can be taken apart and used for other things that are at a reasonable price. Also check out the lumber section of your local home improvement store so pieces of wood that are considered flawed. The prices on these sections of wood are often very discounted and you can usually have the pieces cut down right there if you want/need.

Hack #17: Master 5 essential home remedies.

There will come a time when you're feeling a little (or a lot) under the weather and are desperate to feel better, but you may not want to spend a fortune to get results. Or how about when you have a big date and wake up with a monstrous zit that is deserving of its own zip code. No problem! You can use some home remedies to cure what ails instead. Most home remedies are simple and just as effective as the stuff sitting on store shelves, so why not give it a whirl?

IN A NUTSHELL: Skip the drugstore and opt for home remedies for simple ways to feel and look better. You can use simple, cheap ingredients that you may already have on hand to get rid of that cough or to help ease the discomfort that comes along with the stomach flu.

Why? As long as you're not super sick or have health issues that require you to seek medical attention, you can use home remedies as a substitute for expensive store bought alternatives. Why spend the extra money on something from the store when you're capable of tackling the same problems with stuff from your pantry? I can't think of a reason not to give a try!

I also like to know what I'm putting in and on my body, so that's a pretty good incentive for me use home remedies when possible. There aren't any words that are impossible to pronounce or asterisks for side effects listed on the ingredients used and that's a pretty solid perk in my opinion.

How? There are home remedies available for nearly anything these days and most use items from your fridge or pantry to ease your symptoms. Here are five essential home remedies that will come in handy:

Cough Syrup
Coughs are no fun and can hang around long past the cold they came with. Try a homemade ginger, honey and lemon cough syrup to sooth your throat and quiet that pesky cough. Here's what you'll need and how to make it.

Ingredients:
- *Ginger*
- *Raw honey*
- *2 lemons*
- *Water*
- *A jar for storing*

Peel the ginger root and cut it into slices over a bowl. Zest your lemons over another bowl and set aside. Use a saucepan and add 1 cup of water, ¼ cup of the sliced ginger and about 1 ½ to 2 tablespoons of the lemon zest. Crank up the heat to a boil, then turn it down a bit so it can simmer for 5 minutes. Use a strainer to drain the mixture and set aside. Pour 1 cup of raw honey into a small saucepan and turn the heat on low. Make sure you watch it close and keep it from boiling. Add you ginger solution liquid and the juice from your zested lemons to the honey. Give it a good stir while it simmers on low for about 20 to 30 minutes. It should become thick and syrupy. Now you can pour it into your jar and hopefully cough less. You can take 1 to 2 tablespoons every 4 hours as needed.

Toothache Remedies
Toothaches have a way of generating a type of pain that can't be ignored. While a dentist will most likely need to be seen at some point, a quick bit of pain relief until you can get to one will be super helpful. You'd be

surprised by some of the things that can turn tooth related agony into a nonexistent issue. Try these quick home remedies:

Garlic - A clove of garlic can bring you some serious relief when a toothache attacks. The natural antibiotic properties in garlic help to slow down the effects of bacteria that causes pain. All you need to do is crush up a clove, sprinkle some table salt on it and put it right on the painful tooth. You can even chew on a whole clove if you'd rather. It will work quickly and effectively.

Cloves – This is the mac daddy of all toothache remedies. Cloves have awesome anti-inflammatory, antibacterial, antioxidant and anesthetic abilities. They'll get rid of the pain and help fight off any infection that might be brewing. All you need to do is grind the little guys up, add a bit of coconut oil (or any oil you have) to make a paste. Dab the mixture on the painful area with a cotton ball, Q-tip or your finger to get banish the pain. If you frequently experience tooth pain, go ahead and add some clove oil to a small up of water and use it as a mouth rinse. This will keep infection down and hopefully decrease the pain you experience.

Stomach Flu
The worst of the worst...when a stomach bug hits, there's not much you can do expect stay close to a bathroom and wait it out. There are a few home remedies you can try to relieve some of the symptoms and provide a bit of relief, though. Try these things when your stomach starts rumbling:

Chamomile – This little herb has a lot of great stomach healing properties that will give you relief of symptoms like abdominal cramping, bloating, nausea and gas. To get some relief, add 2 to 3 teaspoons for dried chamomile flowers to a cup of how water and let it steep for about 15 minutes. You can then strain out the flowers before adding a bit of lemon and/or honey to enhance the taste. Try to do this 3 to 4 times a day until you feel better.

Cinnamon – Another anti-bacterial wonder is cinnamon. It will help get rid of the bacteria or virus causing you to feel ill with the added benefit of ridding you of chills and body aches. You can boil cinnamon powder in water and strain it over cheesecloth to make a soothing tea with a bit of honey to aid in the process and enhance the taste. Another option, is to mix a half teaspoon of cinnamon powder with a tablespoon of raw honey with warm water. Drink it and start to feel better.

Sinus Infections
No, the pressure you're feeling in your head and face are not related to the pressures of school, it's more than likely due to a sinus infection. Some sinus infections do require the attention of a doctor, but you can try a few simple home remedies to start. Here are some that I have used:

Herbs – Load up on the hot stuff to dissolve the blockage in your sinuses and to get your nose running. Add cayenne pepper, horseradish, garlic and onion to your meals to start. If that's not getting things moving, add a bit of Wasabi to as well. Just remember that a little of this goes a long way and have some tissues nearby.

Apple Cider Vinegar – When you get those first inklings that a sinus infection is on the horizon, it's time to break out the apple cider vinegar. You'll be able to think out some of the mucus by mixing 1-2 teaspoons of raw, unfiltered apple cider vinegar with 6-8 ounce of water and a teaspoon of raw honey. Toss this concoction back about 3 times a day for a week and you'll hopefully feel some relief.

Acne
We've all been down the acne road and have the scars to prove it. Break outs can occur no matter how well you take care of your skin, but those angry red marks don't have to be that way for as long when you use home remedies. So, the next time you wake up with a zit the size of a dinner plate, give one of these remedies a try

before canceling plans while it heals

Honey – Raw honey will become your new best friend once you see how quickly it speeds up the healing process of those bothersome blemishes. Dip a clean Q-tip in the raw honey and dab it on the area. Leave it on there for about an hour before washing it off with warm water. You can also make a paste with raw honey and cinnamon powder for overnight treatment. You'll wake up with a less redness and swelling.

Ice and Toothpaste Combo – Apply ice to the pimple for a few seconds frequently throughout the day to bring down the swelling. When you're ready for bed, apply white toothpaste to the affected areas and leave it overnight. You'll notice a big difference in the morning and your face will smell minty fresh.

Shortcut: These remedies use a lot of things that you have around the house. If you're prone to certain issues regularly, go ahead and research remedies, make a list of items needed and check your pantry or head to the store to get what's needed. You'll be prepared when the time comes to utilize a home remedy and cut out a delay in relief.

Bonus! Remember, most of these ingredients are used in your kitchen already for cooking and adding them to your food when possible will have some added health benefits that just might keep you from needed a quick fix remedy at times.

Sports and Leisure Hacks

All work and no play...well you know the rest! So, if you want to get up and get moving to blow off some study stink without having to spend a fortune, this is the chapter for you to read and take note of. You can get a workout in and practice some of your new found DIY skills that you learned from the last chapter.

Hack #18: Never pay for a gym.

Getting in a workout is important, especially when you're sitting like a rock studying for hours on end. Despite what you may think, joining a gym is not necessary or even your best option. Save yourself an extra monthly expense and find other ways to work up a sweat.

IN A NUTSHELL: Don't spend money on a gym membership when you can get in a complete workout at home. There are a lot of ways to stay fit and keep your costs down. All it takes is motivation and an internet connection.

Why? Why spend money on a gym membership when there are tons of great workouts you can do at home? Do a quick YouTube or internet search for the kind of exercise you like to do and you're good to go. You can There are hundreds of amazing home workouts on the internet, and some of them are much, much more difficult than a workout you'd get waiting around at a gym.

In other words, you don't need to fork over a bunch of cash to keep in top shape.

How? If you're looking for a workout program that is a little more structured, you can go ahead and invest in a whole series of DVD's (we don't advocate pirating, although that may be an option for the morally questionable college student). This route will cost some money at first, but is still much cheaper in the long run than a gym membership. Plus, you can always sell the program later if you're tired of it and ready to move on to another.

Before you settle on a home workout program to buy, do some research and read reviews from other users. These are some of the workout programs that are said to produce results and seem pretty popular:

- P90X3 – Action packed 30 minute workouts that are super-efficient and intense
- Tracy Anderson: Metamorphosis – 90 day program is geared toward your body type
- Insanity – Sweat drenching, muscle searing workout that lives up to its name
- 10 Minute Trainer – Don't let the short time fool you. After these 10 minutes, you'll be sweating
- Jillian Michaels: Body Revolution – 90 day program with 30 minute daily hardcore videos

Each of these programs is designed to help you shed pounds, lose inches and tone up any soft spots in no time.

Shortcut: Before buying any programs, see if there is a lending library online or on campus. Also check with other students to see if they have anything that would work for you. It's worth a shot if it will save you a few bucks, right?

Additionally, for each of the workouts listed above, there are usually tons and tons of similar workouts online; you just need to do a bit of digging to find them.

Bonus! Check out Reddit for some information about workout programs or for tips to get results. There is a really informative Sub-Reddit for bodyweight training that is super useful and loaded with good stuff, so definitely check it out if you're looking to build some muscles.

Hack #19: Make your own equipment.

Forget all of those infomercials you see late at night for the next big exercise equipment fad. Those things are expensive and usually end up as a place to hang your laundry. Go the simple and cheap route instead by making your own exercise equipment.

IN A NUTSHELL: There's no need to buy exercise equipment when you can make some awesome things out of ordinary items at a cheap price. Get creative with what you have and prepare to work up a sweat.

Why? It's easy to make your own exercise equipment and cheaper than buying it at retail prices. This will make it less of a less if you fall off the workout bandwagon for a bit since you're only shelling out a little cash.

How? You can make a lot of exercise equipment that will suit many exercising styles and needs. Figure out what you're looking for to round out your fitness routine, see if there are any tutorials online to help you get instructions and get building.

Here are some of the DIY fitness equipment that you can make for cheap, with ease and fast:

- Sandbags – All you need is an old duffel bag or rucksack and some pea gravel that has been double bagged with tape reinforcing it to ensure that all of the gravel stays inside. Make a few bags of varying weights to fit your needs across multiple fitness levels.
- Keg weights: Finally, there is a use for all of those kegs after those college ragers! Take the inner device out and fill it with water or sand. You can use it for distance carrying, loading exercises or clean and press.
- Water jug or cinder block hand weights: Don't spend money on dumbells when you can use an old milk jug or cinder blocks instead. All you have to do is rinse out the milk jugs and fill them up with water or sand, instant weights. You can also pick up to cinder blocks from the home improvement store to use as weights instead if that's more your style.
- Punching bag: You can make your own punching bag for super cheap. All you need is a sturdy shell made of canvas or vinyl. If you can get your hands on an old military bag for cheap, do that because those suckers are built to endure the beating you'll be dishing out. They are also already in one piece and won't require sewing. You can line it with foam to help it keep shape if you're not too fond of a lumpy punching bag. Whether it's lined or not, fill it up with free materials that will allow for a bit of give so that it doesn't feel like you hit a wall when punching/kicking it. You can use sawdust, dirt, sand and old rags to get the right amount density. Use a sturdy chain and hook to hang the bag in the right spot. This part may be difficult depending on where you live. Try using a stud finding to find a good anchor for starters.

Shortcut: Make a list of the exercises you'd like to do and what you'll need to do them. This way you can keep an eye out for the materials you need to get started. You'll have a fully loaded workout space in no time.

Bonus! The internet is your friend here, use it. There are tutorials and YouTube videos for all kinds of DIY fitness tools.

Hack #20: Organize some pick-up sports games.

A planned pick-up game on the quad during a break from studying, is a perfect way to get in some exercise, blow off some steam and hang out with your friends. You don't need much to do it and can play for as long or short as you want.

IN A NUTSHELL: All you need is a baseball, football, basket, hockey puck or Frisbee to get a pick-up game going. The space to play is free and the equipment to do so it super cheap. Simply call up your friends and set up the details.

Why: You don't need much to participate in these games, so the cost is pretty much nothing. All you need is something to play and friends to do it with. You don't get much more low maintenance than this as a means to get moving end burn off some stress, pent up energy or that pizza you scarfed down last night.

How: If you're in the mood to toss the ball around for a bit, start texting your friends and have them join you. There's no need to rigid rules or structure in pick-up games and half the fun is the spontaneity of getting together on the fly to play around.

You can make these games a regular event with your friends without any obligation to come if it's not convenient for others. Pick a new game each time you get together based upon what equipment your group already has to avoid having to go buy something new.

Here are some popular pick-up games to give you an idea of what to play and what you'd need to do so:

*   Sandlot ball – This is basically baseball with less structure and the ability to apply any rules you want. You can play anywhere and craft a makeshift field out of whatever you have on hand. You can use anything you want to mark bases and improvise if you're short on balls, bats and gloves.
*   Basketball – All you need here is a hoop and a basketball. You can play a regular game or get creative with the rules if it keeps things interesting.
*   Football – Grab a football and make like Peyton Manning to the park or beach to show your friends how it's done.
*   Frisbee – There are bound to be some wayward Frisbees around campus, so pick one up and start tossing it around. Extra points for the player who knocks the professor's toupee off!
*   Street hockey – Fashion a goal out of whatever is available, find a puck or use a tennis ball and grab some hockey sticks. You've got all you need to play old school game of street hockey.

As you can see, you can play these games anywhere, any time and with anything. Get your friends on board and have fun with it.

Shortcut: If you want to be more organized, you can plan your games out for the month and pre-select the locations. You'll know when and where to meet up, what to bring, who will be there and what to play. If being a bit more structured in your pick up game routine makes things easier for you, more power to you.

Bonus! It's not a bad idea to stock up on some of the cheaper items your group plays with a lot. If you lose a Frisbee or baseball, it's not such a big deal if you'd got a spare on hand. You'll be able to keep playing rather than stopping to go buy a new item or call it a day until the next game.

Thanks! Here's a free gift for you.

As a small token of thanks for buying this book, I'd like to offer a free bonus gift exclusive to my readers:

This action-packed PDF is called *Stress & Students* and has tons of valuable lessons for students who sometimes feel overwhelmed with school. These tips honestly helped keep me sane when I was going through grad school.

In this FREE bonus, you'll learn:
- How to stay focused
- How to keep things in perspective
- What stuff is worth stressing over
- What stuff *isn't* worth stressing over
- How to manage stress when it occurs
- And much more!

You can download the free gift here:
http://www.learnu.org/student-stress/